Help Your 3–5 Year Old Learn to Read

Parents' essentials – friendly books for busy parents
to help their children fulfil their potential.

For full details please send for a free copy of the latest catalogue.
See back cover for address.

Help Your 3–5 Year Old Learn to Read

Ken Adams

PARENTS' ESSENTIALS

Published in 2000 by
How To Books Ltd, 3 Newtec Place,
Magdalen Road, Oxford OX4 1RE, United Kingdom
Tel: (01865) 793806   Fax: (01865) 248780
email: info@howtobooks.co.uk
www.howtobooks.co.uk

British Library Cataloguing in Publication Data.
A catalogue record for this book is available from
the British Library.

Edited by Julie Nelson
Cover design by Shireen Nathoo Design
Produced for How To Books by Deer Park Productions
Typeset by PDQ Typesetting, Newcastle-under-Lyme, Staffordshire
Printed and bound by Hillman Printers, Frome, Somerset

NOTE: The material contained in this book is set out in good faith
for general guidance and no liability can be accepted for loss or
expense incurred as a result of relying in particular circumstances
on statements made in the book. The laws and regulations are
complex and liable to change, and readers should check the current
position with the relevant authorities before making personal
arrangements.

ESSENTIALS *is an imprint of*
How To Books

Contents

Preface

In recent years, there has been a trend favouring parents helping their child with home learning. This has been for all ages – at pre-school, primary and secondary levels. Pre-school children are read to, taught to count, and, in some cases, taught to read. Parents teach the alphabet, read along with their child and teach nursery rhymes and children's songs. Such early learning arouses interest and raises the enjoyment level of learning, and gives a kick start and confidence for when they start school.

Early reading is probably not for every child, but some are definitely ready to read some time before school age. Who are we to deny a bright and inquisitive young learner the joys of finding out about stories and rhymes for themselves? The purpose of this book is to give pointers to parents so that they can help their child to progress in early reading skills, while still maintaining their interest and enjoyment.

Ken Adams

1 How Your Child Learns

For a parent, one of the most crucial aspects of helping a child at home is having some understanding of the how and why of the learning process. This does not need to be a deep knowledge of psychological processes, but rather an appreciation of how your child thinks, particularly at this pre-school age.

Interest in the world around us is one important factor in a child learning well and fast. The encouragement of a parent is another. This means that the parent–child relationship is crucial for early learning success. Some parents have an instinctive feel for what a child's enquiring mind needs. Most parents need some guidance in the form of simple explanations of how to find out what the child knows, and how to build on this rudimentary basis of thinking, while still retaining a child's interest and enjoyment.

REAL-LIFE LEARNING

Almost all of a pre-school child's learning is within real-life experience. It is concrete, as opposed to abstract. Later, abstract learning, through the written word and numbers, will play a much larger part in learning, and the horizons of knowledge will expand much faster, but at this beginning learning phase, verbal word knowledge is built up through experience in real life.

A child learns about colour, form and action, through seeing, touching, tasting and acting out, some time before linking written words with such experiences. They know, for example, what 'run' or 'jump' mean before they can visualise the letters and word form.

This means that one of the most valuable ways in which a parent can help their child is by linking the spoken word to an object or action. Most three-year-olds, for example, should know about a:

spoon	knife	chair	door	window
car	bus	shop	garden	flower

and so on. They should also be able to understand simple instructions such as 'don't touch!', and be aware of the meanings of certain action words:

'run', 'jump', 'eat', 'drink', etc.

FINDING OUT WHAT YOUR CHILD KNOWS

For the purposes of this book, we start at the age of three years. By this age a child will have accumulated a considerable amount of knowledge of the house/garden/shopping environment. However, the range of knowledge between three-year-olds is very great indeed, so it is important to try to assess the word knowledge an individual possesses. Only then can a parent find ways to build on what a child knows. Conversation, obviously at a three-year-old's level, is very effective in achieving this. A parent can discuss what she is doing in the kitchen, the garden, at the supermarket. He or she can talk about a TV programme, a video or a CD Rom, without going too deeply into the whys and wherefores of everyday life.

STEP-WISE LEARNING

This leads on to the basic principles of learning. In general these follow a straightforward pattern. A child's understanding of concepts (like tree, chair, table) are noted mentally in very simple terms. A tree, for example, is 'green, tall, and has a characteristic shape'. There is a simple, rather vague pattern in the child's mind. As time progresses a child may modify this mental pattern – a tree is not like a bush; it has a trunk; some trees have needles, some have leaves, and so on.

Gradually (probably over years) a child's understanding moves from the simple to the complex. There are more concepts in the child's mind as they grow older (e.g. leaf, branch). In addition, there is a trend from thinking in terms of real life towards thinking in terms of symbols (in reading, writing and arithmetic). To ease the transition from lower to higher levels, it is important that a teacher or parent-teacher moves carefully onward and upward in **easy** steps – if the step is too big a learning step, the learner could fail. And this is to be avoided at all costs. A parent can add to the child's understanding only if they introduce knowledge that is not too remote from that understanding. Several short, easy learning steps are better than one big one.

MEMORISING

When talking about memorising with regard to a pre-school

child, we are not usually thinking in terms of repeating times tables. Memorising here is rather familiarising oneself with everyday objects and actions. Some skills are learnt through practice (how to use a spoon) and as understanding develops (the fire is hot), sometimes over a relatively long period of time. Learning is a relaxed, almost imperceptible process, and it is the parent who provides the environment in which these memorising processes take place. Skills, like potty training, are often learnt by repetition, but many **skills** and **meanings** can also be learnt by a process called **pegging**. In pegging, the item or process for memorising is linked to something or someone who captures the child's interest or imagination. For example, counting can be linked to walking up the stairs to bed at night-time and counting the steps, counting cars passing by in the roadway, or counting tins of beans at the supermarket. To link real-life experience with abstract ideas, like counting, particularly at this age, is essential.

CONCENTRATION

This is a word more usually linked with students studying for exams, but it applies equally to three- to five-year olds. Without concentration, there is no **focus** on what is being learnt, and there is little learning. For a parent the aim needs to be to develop an interest in the task to hand, whether a skill, or something to understand. This is why the early stages of reading need to be surrounded by a relaxing and positive environment, so that a child will link an extremely pleasant experience with the learning of reading. The accompaniment to the reading experience is generally by a parent who provides a sense of security, perhaps reading a story to their child just before bedtime, maybe acting out a character, and talking about what can be seen in the pictures.

2 Introducing Your Child to Books

You need to include a wider area of understanding in which words, actions, and discussions are involved:

finger rhymes	ABC books	nursery rhymes
fairy stories	songs	riddles
non-fiction books	picture books	other story books

Introduce books to extend a child's knowledge and understanding of the world. Use both the spoken and written word, and pictures.

Pre-school children can find out about science, geography and history (including local geography and local history) and an even wider range of subjects from illustrated books, TV, videos, CD Roms and the Internet. This applies equally to written stories in books, which are highly illustrated, and even animated. A parent should take the role of animator, by acting out parts in a story or rhyme, and of narrator, by talking about illustrations in story books.

FINGER RHYMES
Children become intrigued by rhymes at a very young age (when babies, very often), so by the age of three, many toddlers know several rhymes. One of the most universally known is:

'Round and round the garden like a Teddy Bear, one step, two steps, tickly under there....'

I watch Andrew at 15 months being taught this rhyme at his parent's knee, and also Sonia in a Muslim family at the same age. The enjoyment of both is evident. 'Do again,' says Sonia.

The rhythm of rhymes is important, and music is an important background to an early interest in books. To illustrate how young a child can be when first interested in music and rhythm, Tiffany at just two months would rock backwards and forwards in perfect time to pop music.

An early introduction to words and books is therefore helped by the acting out of rhymes and riddles like:

- 'Round and round the garden'
- 'This little piggy went to market'
- '1, 2, 3, 4, 5, Once I caught a fish alive, 6, 7, 8, 9, 10, Then I let it go again'
- 'Pat a cake'
- 'Two little dickie birds'
- 'Incey wincey spider'
- 'Hickory Dickory Dock'
- 'Humpty Dumpty'
- 'Baa, baa black sheep'
- 'London Bridge is falling down'
- 'Jack and Jill'
- 'This old man'
- 'Little Miss Muffet'

The tunes are appealing, and there are actions as well as the rhyme, together with a story, of sorts, to that rhyme. Finger rhymes and nursery rhymes make a good beginning to getting interested in books (see the companion volume *Help Your Child Learn Through Rhymes, Riddles and Songs*).

BOOKS FOR LEARNING

For three- to five-year-olds these include:

- ABC books

and books about:

- the farm
- the seaside
- shops
- the zoo, and so on.

They often have no words, or perhaps just one word on the page. Some of these books are badly organised, and badly presented. Others, from reputable publishers, are very valuable starter books for a toddler to have as 'my book', to carry around as he or she plays. Very small children (eighteen months to two years old) have board books, material books or 'bath' books (which stand being wetted in bath play).

John and Tiffany had these type of books as babies, and could truly be said to have 'grown up' with books.

Books such as those mentioned above are invaluable both

for extending knowledge, and for providing a talking point:

'Look, the tractor has two big wheels at the back, and two small ones at the front.'

'Cows give us milk to drink.'

STORY BOOKS

For this age group, story books will extend from fairy stories to abridged classics. Since a parent sits with their child and reads the story, the choice of story book depends on storyline and illustrations. Good characters are essential, because children of this age seem to cling to the characters above all else. This is the reason for the universal success of fairy stories:

Little Red Riding Hood	The Gingerbread Man
Goldilocks	Chicken Licken
Snow White	Jack and the Beanstalk
Cinderella	The Sleeping Beauty
The Three Little Pigs	

Shortened versions of these tales with big, brightly coloured pictures will greatly fire your child's imagination, particularly if you, the parent, act out each story.

READING WITH YOUR CHILD

Getting your three-year-old interested in reading is probably the most important input that you as a parent can give to your child's education. For this reason, a daily reading period needs to be treated as a very special time, when your child is relaxed and feeling secure. Most parents choose bedtime as the best time to read a small story book, but any part of the day is a good time, as long as there is no element of coercion in it. When you sit with your child, occasionally trace the words you read with your finger, without any attempt to teach reading. Besides indicating that the story is within the words, this action also shows your child that you are reading from left to right.

3 Letter Sounds

In the learning of reading, there is what might be termed a common-sense sequence of events that needs to be followed by the learner before becoming a skilled reader. The order of events can be juggled a little, but basically a reader will often identify words from the starting letter, and from the shape of the word. For new words, they will also need to piece together the shapes and sounds of letters to try to elicit the overall sound of a word. This is called 'phonics', and it can happily account for many early words that a child meets, such as:

man   hat   stamp

It is a good basis from which to approach reading, as long as a parent realises that their child will meet many words that do not fit into the 'system'.

'Car' is a simple word, but the 'a' in 'car' is not sounded like the 'a' in 'apple', for example.

There are also combinations of vowels that defy attempts to fit them into the phonic structure:

pear   pair

However, it is extremely useful to build a child's reading around a skeleton of phonics. You begin by defining the sounds of the letters in the alphabet:

a is for apple

b is for ball

This can then progress to three-letter words that have the standard vowel sounds:

c – a – t

m – a – n

c – u – p

Clearly, this limits the range of words that can be used in stories. The language can be rather stilted. However, taken on balance, children learn to read faster if there is a structured system, which can be built on, seeing words with unusual sounds as idiosyncrasies, exceptions to the system, rather than as part of the pattern.

ALPHABET LETTERS

One of the most important aspects of reading that a starter reader needs to grasp is the recognition of the first letter of a word. For this reason, the phonic alphabet is vital:

a is for apple, ant

b is for bed, bat, bin, bun, bag

c is for cat, cot, cap

d is for dog, dot

e is for egg, elephant

f is for fox

g is for gate, gun

h is for hat

i is for insect, ink

j is for jam, jet

k is for kite

l is for ladder

m is for man, mat, mum

n is for nut

o is for ox, orange

p is for pot, parrot, pin, pig

qu is for queen

r is for rat, rabbit, rug

s is for sun

t is for top, tap

u is for umbrella

v is for van, vest

w is for window, wall

x as in box

y is for yacht

z is for zebra

The system is far from perfect. Trying to find simple words with the correct vowel sounds that represent real-life objects, and which are also within a pre-school child's experience, is difficult. Not many three-year-olds for example, know what a rug or a top (spinning) is. Since it is important that words are pegged to their real-life equivalent to ensure understanding and memorising, words at this stage must have their picture equivalent.

a is for apple

EMPHASISING LETTER SHAPE AND SOUND

To ensure efficient memorising of letter shape and sound, links with real life need to be established. You can draw the letters large on a sheet of paper, or trace the letters in a tray half full of sand. Relating the letter shapes to real-life shapes can be very effective:

a is like an apple

b is like a boot

c is like a cup on its side

d is like a duck

e is like sleepy eyes

f is like a tall man bending over

g is like a goldfish

h is like a running man

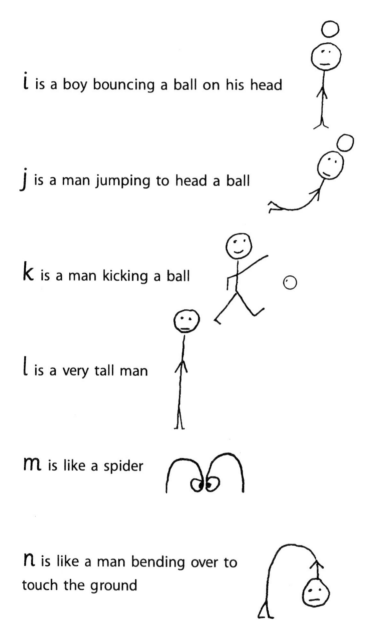

i is a boy bouncing a ball on his head

j is a man jumping to head a ball

k is a man kicking a ball

l is a very tall man

m is like a spider

n is like a man bending over to touch the ground

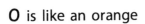

o is like an orange

p is a lollipop in a stick

q is a lollipop with a string attached

r is a walking stick

s is a snake (making a hissing sound)

t is like a man sitting down

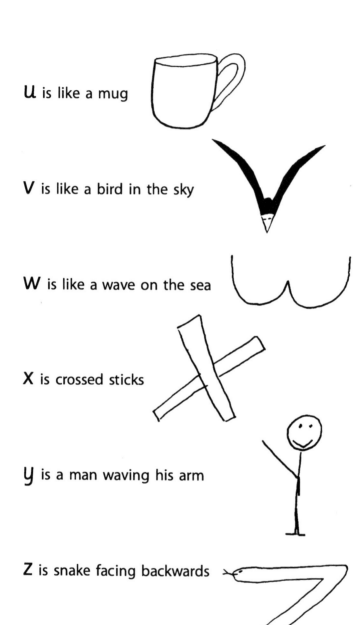

u is like a mug

V is like a bird in the sky

W is like a wave on the sea

X is crossed sticks

y is a man waving his arm

Z is snake facing backwards

It is important not to stretch a point here. If a child cannot see the connection between the letter shape and real-life form, then it is best to be content with tracing the shape, and repeating the letter sound. However, some representations work well. The **S** for **snake** is very effective, as is the 'three-fingered' **spider**, **m**.

LEARNING LETTER SOUNDS TAKES TIME

Learning phonics should not be approached with excessive zeal, but rather it needs to be incorporated into pre-reading activities as an extra game or two. At most, five letters can be concentrated on at one time, and often letter sounds are taught one at a time, picking out the letters from text, from advertisements, even from videos and computer software.

4 Word Building

The words that a child reads in starter reading books are generally in one of three categories:

- The first are those words built on a solid **phonic base**:

  r – u – n   c – a – t   m – a – n   s – u – n

- In the second category are those words that are much **used in text**. It is difficult, in fact, to write a reasonable story without including them:

flower	house	garden	car	school
boat	boy	doll	baby	snow, etc.

  They refer to concrete objects, so that illustrations can 'show' the word, and, in general, such words are learnt relatively easily.

- More difficult are those in the third category. They are **abstract**, and it is impossible to write sentences without many of them:

they	is	in	a	the
he	was	here	there	on
she	and	go	to	am

  It is extremely hard to get a small child to memorise these

as separate words, and their learning is best left to the sentence-building stage, when a child can learn them almost imperceptibly, through repetition in reading. However, 'is', 'in', 'on', 'and', and 'am' have phonic structures, so are learnt reasonably quickly.

BUILDING SIMPLE PHONIC WORDS

Once the phonic sounds to the letters are known, simple three-letter words representing concrete objects can be built up. Ideally, the letters can be written on square portions of card, and then cut out. Learning can involve one vowel at a time:

'a' words ('a' as in 'ant')

m	a	n
c	a	t
h	a	t
d	a	d

h	a	m
j	a	m
c	a	p
t	a	p

'e' words ('e' as in 'egg')

p	e	n
t	e	n
b	e	d
l	e	g

'i' words ('i' as in 'in')

b	i	n
p	i	n
t	i	n
p	i	g
l	i	p

'o' words ('o' as in 'orange')

c	o	t
d	o	g

'u' words ('u' as in 'umbrella')

b	u	n
g	u	n
s	u	n
n	u	t
m	u	g
m	u	m
c	u	p

Later, these words can be combined with **key words** (most used words) to make complete sentences:

'Here is a cup and a mug.'

'The dogs runs in the garden.'

'The boy plays in the sun.'

LINKING WITH REAL LIFE

So far, all learning for reading has been by linking concrete objects or actions with letters or simple words. The concrete objects can either be to hand (the 'sun' is in the sky, and can be pointed out, a 'cup' is on the table), or pictures can be drawn (e.g. of a 'pig').

After you have spent time word-building in the above fashion, test your child by asking them to link word with picture in the following:

Draw a line to the picture:

bus

cup

hat

cat

dot

pin

box

sun

tap

van

ten

fox

zip

leg

dog    bat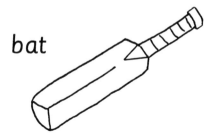

Other words can be linked:

apple    car

house    boat

flower    tree

5 Sentence Building

The final stage in the sequence from recognising letters to reading simple story books is forming simple sentences. For this the **words** are **cut-outs**, and they are joined together to make sentences.

Example

is pieced together as:

Such sentences, simply put together with the picture, tell a story. To create a character, we can add the name of the dog:

> this is Biff
> Biff runs up the road

or the beginnings of a fairy story:

> 'Here is an old woman.
> She makes a gingerbread man.
> She lets him out.
> The gingerbread man runs away.
> "Run, run, as fast as you can,
> you can't catch me,
> I'm the gingerbread man."'

The rhyme is repeated several times in the story and the starter reader becomes familiar with words like 'fast', 'catch', 'you', etc. Rereading of the story usually leads to the learning of difficult words, but there are some children who do not respond very quickly to this simplistic approach, and need some further help in memorising non-phonic words.

LOOK-AND-SAY WORDS

It helps with the learning of words that do not have a phonic structure if these are written on cards and learnt as **flash cards**. In this method your child is learning to recognise the shape of the word. A whole range of words can be learnt in this manner, making a game of going through the cards after reading a story to your child (see the story sections at the end of this book). It helps if they can recognise a phonic part of a word, and, of course, if the starter letter is recognised. Action words are often learnt at this stage:

It cannot be stressed too greatly that a parent should not labour over flash cards. They need to form only a small part of a reading time, or your child may associate an unpleasant experience with story reading, something which is greatly to be avoided. With a relaxed and easy-going attitude by the parent, however, flash cards can be very helpful for some children.

PARTS OF THE BODY AND ACTION WORDS

An early reader will come across words that describe parts of the face, the body, and clothes:

| eye | nose | ear | hair | mouth |
| arm | leg | tummy | hand | foot |

socks

skirt

dress

vest

shoe

coat

Here are some key action words:

drink eat

sleep  swim

drive  sit

walk

MAKING SENTENCES FROM ACTION WORDS

As with the single words, short sentences can be linked with a picture that describes what is happening:

the boy swims

she jumps

he runs to school

the baby eats his food

she drinks her milk

dad sleeps on the bed

mum drives the car

she walks home

the dog sits on the chair

Each sentence tells a story, and the picture confirms what the words tell us. After telling a story through a simple sentence, the next phase is to build into full story-form by joining together several picture-sentences. This pattern is followed in the next chapter.

6 Reading Simple Stories

In this chapter, simplified versions of fairy stories have been chosen as examples of simple stories through which an early reader can consolidate their progress. The simplified stories used here are:

- The Gingerbread Man (with pictures)
- Goldilocks and the Three Bears (with pictures)
- Little Red Riding Hood
- Jack and the Beanstalk

THE GINGERBREAD MAN

1. the old woman makes a gingerbread man

2. he jumps off the table and runs

3.   'come back!'
     says the old woman

4.   'run, run as fast as
     you can, you can't
     catch me, I'm the
     gingerbread man'

5.   a dog says 'come back!'

6.   'run run ...'
     (finish the words)

7. a horse says
   'come back!'

8. 'run, run...'

9. the gingerbread
   man gets to a river

10. 'I will help you to get
    over' says the fox

11. the gingerbread man
    jumps on his back

12. 'jump on my nose'
    says the fox

13. the fox throws the
    gingerbread man into
    the air and eats him up

Flash cards for this story can be for these words:

come   back   old   woman   horse   dog

says   you   will   help   air   can't

GOLDILOCKS AND THE THREE BEARS

1. here are the three bears

2. there is baby bear, mummy bear and daddy bear

3. they go for a walk

4. here is Goldilocks she goes in the house

5. she tries daddy bear's porridge
    'it is too hot' she says

6. she tries mummy bear's porridge
    'it is too cold' she says

7. she tries baby bear's porridge
    'this is good' she says
    she eats it all up

8. Goldilocks goes upstairs

9. she tries daddy bear's bed
   'it is too hard' she says

10. she tries mummy bear's bed
    'it is too soft' she says

11. she tries baby bear's bed
    'this is good' she says

12. she goes to sleep

13. **the bears come back**

14. **'my porridge is all gone'
     says baby bear**

15. **they go upstairs**

16. **'a girl is in my bed'
     says baby bear**

17. Goldilocks runs away

For this story it may help to prepare **flash cards** for the following words:

Goldilocks	**here**	**come**	**away**	**porridge**
upstairs	**all**	**sleep**	**goes**	**soft**
hard	**good**	**gone**	**says**	**tries**
too	**baby**	**mummy**	**daddy**	**bear**
cold	**house**			

RED RIDING HOOD

1. this is Red Riding Hood
2. she is taking food to her grandma
3. the wolf sees her
4. he runs to grandma's house
5. grandma hides
6. the wolf dresses up like grandma
7. Red Riding Hood sees the wolf

8.   'what big eyes you have grandma,' says Red Riding Hood
9.   'all the better to see you with,' says the wolf
10. 'what big teeth you have grandma,' says Red Riding Hood
11. 'all the better to eat you with,' says the wolf
12. he runs after Red Riding Hood
13. Red Riding Hood's grandad runs after the wolf
14. Red Riding Hood is safe

Words for use as **flash cards**:

safe	**after**	**grandma**	**grandad**
Red Riding Hood	**wolf**	**teeth**	**her**
eyes	**what**	**dresses**	**like**
hides	**house**	**taking**	**food**

JACK AND THE BEANSTALK

1.   Jack is poor
2.   he sells his cow for some beans
3.   his mother is cross
4.   she throws the beans in the garden
5.   next day a beanstalk has grown
6.   Jack climbs up the beanstalk
7.   at the top is a giant's castle
8.   the giant comes
9.   Jack hides
10. the giant counts his gold
11. 'fee, fi, fo, fum,' he says
12. the giant sleeps

13. Jack runs away with the gold
14. the giant runs after him
15. Jack climbs down the beanstalk
16. he chops the beanstalk down
17. the giant falls to the ground

Flash cards can be made for the following words:

poor	**some**	**sells**	**mother**
cross	**throws**	**garden**	**next**
beanstalk	**grown**	**climbs**	**giant**
castle	**hides**	**counts**	**comes**
sleeps	**gold**	**after**	**chops**
down	**falls**	**ground**	

7 More Phonics and Other Essentials

A further difficulty in early reading is the presence of double consonants at the beginning of a word – e.g. **br** or **bl**, **cr** or **cl** – which need to be said as one letter. Words with such beginnings include:

black	**brick**	**bread**
clock	**crab**	
drink		
flower	**frog**	
grass	**glove**	
pram	**plug**	
step	**sleep**	**spot** **swing** **shop**
train		

There are also double blends in word middles:

moon   **spoon**   **feet**

One effective way of emphasising these double consonants and blends is to point them out as you read stories to your child. This need not be too obvious, just a passing remark: 'This is **cl** for clock.'

There is a difficult balance to strike between reading for pure enjoyment, and learning the mechanics of reading. Some children learn reading skills through reading along with someone, but for others this is very difficult to achieve. What seems to be most effective is to include mostly pure reading sessions with a little of the mechanics (phonics, look and say) before or afterwards. Making the letters a game format can be very appealing.

GAMES FOR PHONICS

These can be played as a child is learning phonics. For example, when learning 'c' for cut you can point out other objects in the room that begin with that letter – card, cot, etc. On another day you can then say, 'Find me something that begins with "c".'

When your child knows his or her phonics well, you can play 'I spy with my little eye, something beginning with "b".' If your child knows colours, then you can ask 'I spy with my little eye, a colour beginning with "y",' and this gives a good measure of success to what can be a difficult game for this age.

Word-building games where, say, 'c', 'u' and 'p' are out of order, and you say 'find out what the word says when the letters are in the right order' can be surprisingly difficult, so be patient. This game is effectively a test of spelling, and you will need to help your child quite a bit at first.

Sentence-making games suit only the very best readers, who are given cards with words on, and are asked to put them into a reasonable order.

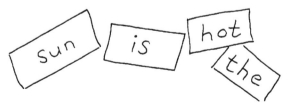

In general, a rule of thumb for activities is to try an activity for two or three minutes, and if it is obviously too difficult for your child, leave it for some later date.

BOOKS FOR PROGRESSING READERS

Essential for pre-school children who are beginning to read are books which have relatively simple language and bright, colourful and interesting pictures. It also goes without saying that there should be interesting characters and a good *idea* to the book (or story). Picture books are nowadays produced in abundance, and range from the plainly terrible to the positively brilliant. Humour is a strong element in many. Many cater for the pre-reader (and have no words) or beginning reader, and others for the advancing reader. For example:

- *The Very Hungry Caterpillar*, Eric Cole
- *Spot* series, Eric Hill
- *The Snowman*, Raymond Briggs
- *Nursery Collection*, Shirley Hughes
- *Old Bear*, Jane Hissey
- *Not Now, Bernard*, David McKee
- *Kipper*, Mick Inkpen
- *Where the Wild Things Are*, Maurice Sendak
- *Happy Families/Funnybones* series, Allan Ahlberg
- *Elephant Family* series, Jill Murphy
- *Gorilla*, Anthony Browne
- *When I Was Your Age*, Ken Adams

There are many others. Many of the older books are in libraries. There are also board and pop-up books, which perhaps add little to reading skills, but do add to the general enjoyment of books.

JOURNEYS, WORDS AND WRITING

Knowledge of words and word meanings is greatly increased by trips to places like the seaside, the supermarket, the fair or the zoo, as long as you, the parent, make a conscious effort to discuss and inform. At the seaside and the fair, for example, there are:

fish	**boats**	**ships**	**the sea**	**sand**
stones	**shells**	**waves**	**a pier**	**roundabouts**
slides	**river rides**	**log flumes**	**big wheels**	**flashing lights**

Perhaps your child can include such things in a picture or stick words on card, or try to write words that define or express what they have seen. Experience is expanded, and often, with it, intelligence and reading ability.

OPPOSITES

A knowledge of these also helps the understanding of words:

up	down
over	under
hot	cold
big	little

fat	thin
fast	slow
wet	dry
happy	sad
laugh	cry
hard	soft

Your child now begins to move into the more abstract world, extending understanding even further.

WRITING AND PICTURES

As your child's reading ability develops, they will want to write about what they experience, however simple the words used. The reading system advocated in this book is multi-sensory, and includes a variety of methods, and learning to write words and sentences helps to extend reading ability. To help, you can assist with the writing of words your child wishes to write on cards, with pictures they have drawn, in scrapbooks or records of visits. It is well to bear in mind, though, that any writing for most children of this age is difficult, and copying is the main avenue of expression for some time.

8 Developments at Different Ages

THE THREE YEAR OLD CHILD

- Controls the direction in which a pencil or crayon moves. Can write an X, draw a circle or write C.
- Can build up to nine wooden bricks high.
- Can order objects in long lines.
- Can fit, sort and match various shapes, including jigsaw puzzle pieces – usually no more than 15–20 pieces – by three and a half years.

Even by this age the range of abilities is considerable. John at three and a half years had enthusiastically tried many activities, and was very advanced in maths, could read and write exceptionally well, and played chess and the piano. Others know some colours, and can count a little – they are often more interested in purely physical activities, but still love to be read to at bedtime. Most talk incessantly, although a few talk late, and still catch up with their precocious friends. Usually, pre-school children have a highly developed sense of humour, and can often memorise rhymes and songs perfectly. Some have been helped by very knowledgeable parents, who value play and their child's interest in learning, particularly reading.

Toys for this age group that can assist reading include alphabet learning desks, writing desks, crayons and drawing paper, stencils and templates, alphabet floor puzzles, educational videos and CDs, and talking story books.

THE FOUR YEAR OLD CHILD

- Becoming very competent at copying words and numbers.
- Can cut out well with scissors, and likes making scrapbooks.
- Some children can write down their name and other words.
- Some remember words with ABC books, and a few can read a little.
- Very interested in imaginative and humorous stories, including fairy stories and well-written stories in picture books. Interesting pictures are a strong focus.

Suitable **toys** include word-matching games, ABC wall charts, charts including days of the week and months of the year. Information books for children become of great interest, particularly where they are highly illustrated. Printing sets often hold a temporary fascination.

Songs for this age available on cassette, CD, CD Rom and videos, include:

Yankee Doodle	Skip to my Lou
She'll be coming round the mountain	Lil' Liza Jane
Bananas in pyjamas	I know an old lady
Michael Finnegan	Farmer's in his den
This old Man	A'roving
Lil' brown jug	Blow the man down
Merrily we roll along	Scarborough Fair
Oh, soldier, soldier	Donkey riding
Sing a Rainbow	Campdown Races
Go tell Aunt Rhody	Here we go looby lou

Hokey cokey

I'd like to teach the world to sing

Miss Polly had a dolly who was
    sick, sick, sick

Skye boat song

Cockles and mussels

Danny Boy

Poems include:

- *The Owl and the Pussycat*, Edward Lear
- *Matilda*, Hilaire Belloc
- *Adventures of Isabel*, Ogden Nash
- *What is Pink?*, Christina Rossetti.

This poem is useful for reading *by* an early reader as well as for reading *to* them:

Teddy Bear's Playtime

> Monday morning, Postman Ted,
> Weigh the parcels, sort the mail,
> Envelopes and stamps for sale.
> Count the letters up to ten
> Then we play this game again.
> When it's dark you go away
> To come and play another day.
>
> Tuesday morning, Busman Ted,
> Board the bus and climb the stairs,
> Ding the bell, collect the fares.
> Count the bus stops up to ten

Then we play this game again.
When it's dark you go away
To come and play another day.

Wednesday morning, Shopman Ted,
Stack the tins and ring the till,
Give the customer his bill.
Count the money up to ten
Then we play this game again.
When it's dark you go away
To come and play another day.

Thursday morning, Trainman Ted,
Fill the train from front to back,
Blow the whistle round the track.
Count the stations up to ten
Then we play this game again.
When it's dark you go away
To come and play another day.

Friday morning, Policemen Ted,
Guide the traffic, walk the beat,
Guard the bank that's in High Street.
Count the robbers up to ten
Then we play this game again.
When it's dark you go away
To come and play another day.

Saturday morning, Doctor Ted,
Give the pills for coughs and sneezes,
Bandage bones and cure diseases.
Count the patients up to ten
Then we play this game again.
When it's dark you go away
To come and play another day.

Sunday morning, Rest-day Ted,
Put our feet up, watch TV,
Read the paper, have some tea.
Count our fingers up to ten
Till we play this game again.
When it's dark this time you'll stay
Tomorrow is another day.

Ken Adams, *You Can Be Your Child's Best Teacher*

Videos and films include:
- most Disney films
- *The Wizard of Oz*
- *Bedknobs and Broomsticks*
- *Chitty Chitty Bang Bang*.

THE FIVE YEAR OLD CHILD

By the age of five years, when many children are assessed for school entrance, most should have a knowledge of counting, some awareness of reading words, particularly those of special importance in real life (DANGER, EXIT), and some writing ability (knowing their name, for example).

At this age, your child is becoming very competent physically:

- They can dress and undress themselves, can often do up their laces, brush their teeth, comb their hair, and wash and bath themselves.

- Reading written numbers leads to using the telephone.

- They can now draw a recognisable man.

- The sense of time duration is getting good, and the ability to construct stories improves rapidly.

Board games help both reading and maths (e.g. junior versions of well-known games). Some **computer educational games** are useful.